VIA Folios 92

Ancestors' Song

Poems by Maria Mazziotti Gillan

OTHER BOOKS BY MARIA MAZZIOTTI GILLAN

Flowers from the Tree of Night, Chantry Press, 1980

Winter Light, Chantry Press, 1985

Luce D'Inverno, Cross-Cultural Communications, 1987

The Weather of Old Seasons, Cross-Cultural Communications, 1987

Taking Back My Name, Malafemmina Press, 1990; Lincoln Springs Press, 1991, repeated printings

Where I Come From: Selected and New Poems, Guernica Editions, 1995, 1997

Things My Mother Told Me, Guernica Editions, 1999

Italian Women in Black Dresses, Guernica Editions, 2002, 2003, 2004

Maria Mazziotti Gillan: Greatest Hits 1972-2002, Pudding House Publications, 2003

Talismans/Talismani, Ibiskos Editions, 2006

All That Lies Between Us, Guernica Editions, 2007

Nightwatch, Poems by Maria Mazziotti Gillan and Aeronwy Thomas, The Seventh Quarry Press, 2010

Moments in the Past That Shine, The Ridgeway Press, 2010

What We Pass On: Collected Poems: 1980-2009, Guernica Editions, 2010

The Place I Call Home, NYQ Books, 2012

Writing Poetry to Save Your Life: How to Find the Courage to Tell Your Stories, MiroLand, Guernica, 2013

The Silence in an Empty House, NYQ Books, 2013

Ancestors' Song

Poems by Maria Mazziotti Gillan

BORDIGHERA PRESS

Library of Congress Control Number: 2013947909

COVER ART: "Sometimes You Sing"
acrylic on paper, 8.5 x 11
by Al Tacconelli

Photograph of author courtesy of Joseph Costa
www.joecphoto.com

Printed in the United States.

Published by
BORDIGHERA PRESS
John D. Calandra Italian American Institute
25 West 43rd Street, 17th Floor
New York, NY 10036

VIA FOLIOS 92
ISBN 978-1-59954-063-4

For my mother, Angelina Schiavo Mazziotti,
and my father, Arturo Mazziotti
In gratitude, for their unwavering support and love

ACKNOWLEDGMENTS

Grateful acknowledgments to the editors of the following journals in which these poems, sometimes in earlier versions, first appeared, or are forthcoming: "I Open a Box," *Narrativenortheast.com*, 2013; "Summer Evenings Under the Grape Arbor," *Meadowlandsmuse.com*, 2013; "Clementines," *The Lantern Lit*, August 2013; "I Was the Girl Who Never Spoke," *New Jersey English Journal*, 2009; "What Did I Want," *Paddlefish*, 2013; "Little House on the Prairie," *Solo Café*, 2013; "Going to the Rivoli in Downtown Paterson," "My Father Worked the Third Shift," and "Ancestors' Song," *Lips*, 2012; "Sleepover," *Prairie Schooner*, Summer 2013; "The Cigar Factories in Yuba City, Florida" and "This Is a Love Song, a Work Song, a Song of Grief," *Lips*, 2013; "Riding a Harley with James Dean," *Lips*, 2009; "Why Is It When I think of You," *Passages North*, Winter 2013; "They Call It Fracking," *Evolutionary Review*, 2012 and Eco Poetry Feature, *PoetsUSA.com*, 2012; "New Jersey Poem," *Evolutionary Review, 2012*; "Lisa Montgomery Speaks," *Louisiana Literature*, 2007; "Rapunzel," *Rattle*; "What Protects Us," *San Diego Poetry Annual*, 2013-14; "My Mother's Mulberry Trees," "Manhattan Cab Story," "At the Breakfast Table," "Changing My Name," "Traveling Long Distances," "When the Factory Whistle Blows," "You Need to Change," *San Diego Poetry Annual*, 2014-15; "*Biancheria* and My Mother," *Lips*, 2013 and *Embroidered Stories Anthology*, 2013; "After My Reading in New York City," "Poem on Our 45th Anniversary," and "Sometimes I Feel As Though I'm Back in the Sixth Grade," *Lips*, 2014; My Mother Tells Us Stories of San Mauro, *Poet to Poet NightWatch*, Swansea, Wales, 2010 and *Collaborative Vision: the Poetic Dialogue Project Anthology*, 2009.

TABLE OF CONTENTS

Ancestors' Song

I OPEN A BOX

…and find inside a picture,
of myself as a child, sitting
on a small chair, wearing overalls
and shoes that must have been
hand-me-downs because they are
so worn the sole is coming loose.
I am no more than 18 months
old and cannot have been walking
all that long. I am squinting
into the sun, my nose crinkling
with effort the way it crinkles now
when I am trying to see in bright light.
Behind me, the six-family tenement
where I was born on 5th Avenue
in Paterson, the rickety stairs rise up
three floors, the porches tilt a bit
as though they might fall off
if someone were to jump on them
too hard. My mother delivered
me herself in this coldwater flat.
The doctor didn't get to her in time,
and when he did, he, in his pressed
and starched white shirt and expensive
suit and polished shoes, stood at the door
and didn't enter the room. My mother
cut the cord and washed me off, wrapped
me in a clean blanket. When she
was dying years later, she said,
"The doctor didn't even come into
the room. He washed his hands, wiped
them on one of the rough linen towels
I brought from Italy, stood in the doorway.
"You'll be okay," he said, and left.

"Oh, well," my mother said, "I think he was afraid of catching it."
"Catching what?" I asked.
"Poverty," she said.

Summer Evenings Under the Grape Arbor

Summer evenings under the grape arbor,
my mother gave us tangerines
and homemade lemonade.
She had a juice squeezer made of thick glass
and a fat glass pitcher and she'd press the lemons
on the pointed top of the squeezer. The pits would remain
behind while the juice fell through the slots into the pitcher.
Then she'd add water and sugar and ice and stir and put it
in the ice box to cool. We'd sit in the evenings
at the oilcloth-covered table under the arbor,
and she'd give us a glass of lemonade and a tangerine to peel
and eat. The air was full of the tangy aroma of the tangerines
on our skin, and we'd play gin rummy and talk and laugh
until it was nearly too dark to see anymore, the air full
of fireflies that circled us like tiny falling stars.

CLEMENTINES

The pungent aroma of clementines lingers on my hands
long after I have peeled the skin off them. The perfume
of the fruit carries me back to my mother's kitchen
in the apartment on 17th Street when my mother
peeled a tangerine for me, encouraging me,
her sickly, skinny seven-year-old daughter to eat.
My mother, hands quick and efficient, peeled
the fruit and fed me one section at a time.

When I was a grown woman with children of my own,
my mother sat with me at her kitchen table and sliced
an apple for me, passing me one slice at a time,
and my daughter, grown up now too, remembers
her grandmother cutting up an orange or an apple
and feeding it to her when she was a child. My mother
never learned how to read and write English.
When she wanted to go to night school, my father said,
"No, women don't need to go to school," but my mother
knew by instinct how to love, knew how to nurture plants
and children so they'd thrive, knew how to offer
the right word of comfort, the words to give us courage
even when we were most afraid. No school could have
taught her what she knew. She taught us how to
reach out to others and feed them
one slice of comfort at a time.

WHAT IS THIS SORROW THAT NEVER LEAVES

What is this sorrow that never leaves, the space inside us
that nothing can fill? When I was a little girl my mother
took us to Dr. R's office on River Street in Paterson
when we got sick. I was sick a lot. Dr. R. practiced
in the ghetto where he got paid with crumpled five dollar
bills, or with five dollars in change, or where sometimes

he didn't get paid at all, though we heard he lived
in a mansion in Franklin Lakes and did okay
off those crumpled immigrant dollars. I was sick
every other week, bronchitis, and fevers and no one
ever mentioned allergies as a cause but Dr. R. had
a fluoroscope machine. It was magic. He'd stand me
behind it and he could see all my bones. What that
was supposed to show him about 105 degree fevers
and hacking coughs I don't know, but it impressed
the Italians of Riverside who thought he must be able
to diagnose anything with that fluoroscope machine.

What is this sorrow that never leaves, the space inside us
that nothing can fill? I think of going to downtown Paterson
to buy shoes and slipping my feet into a machine they had
in the shoe department at Jacob's Department Store.
I'd slip off my shoes, slide my feet into that machine.
It seemed to be a fluoroscope machine for feet, because
I swear I remember seeing all the little bones in my toes.

What is this sorrow that never leaves, the empty spaces
that nothing can fill? If we could go back to Dr. R's, if his
office was still there, if his fluoroscope machine still worked,
if all of this wasn't fifty years ago, would I be able to see
the bones of this sorrow, the shape and texture of all
that we long for and cannot ever name?

ZIA LOUISA AND THE CHOCOLATE SQUARES

Zia Louisa, my honorary aunt, had no children of her own
and refused to take in her husband's son so he lived
with distant relatives of his mother. How he must have hated
Zia Louisa, who let him live in her second floor apartment
for two days before she told her husband she would not have
the boy in her house anymore. Zia Louisa must have weighed
250 pounds, held in by one of those old whalebone corsets
with bone stays and laces. She dyed her hair
a brassy red, wore bright lipstick and makeup, was always
busy and working hard, I never remember seeing her sit still.
She loved to dance the Tarantella at Cilentana Society
dances, and she had a little fine handkerchief she'd use
to wipe away the sweat. After her first three husbands died,
she married her fourth, Zio Guillermo, that handsome
silver-haired man who became my godfather. They were
an unlikely pair. Zio Guillermo, so soft spoken, so gentle,
so kind, and Zia Louisa, so outspoken and brash.

When we'd visit Zia Louisa in her two-family house on 18th
Street, she'd serve the adults espresso and anisette
and homemade cookies. For the children, she poured glasses
of milk with a drop of coffee and sugar and then she'd go
to her china cupboard, open the glass doors, and draw out one
of those large bars of Hershey's chocolate, and break off one
thick square for each of us. My mother made everything
herself. She never bought chocolate bars or Oreos or
Creamsicles, so Zia's chocolate square was an exquisite
pleasure, one we savored as long as we could, holding it in
our mouths until it melted away.

Before they bought the house on 18th Street, they lived
on the second floor of our house on 17th. My mother
said in the night she'd hear Zia Louisa sobbing. The next

morning Zia Louisa would come downstairs cheerful
and laughing, pretending nothing had happened during the night.
Years later my mother tells me she didn't know what was
wrong. What I remember most about Zia Louisa, even now,
is the mystery that cloaked that anguished sobbing
in the night, and the way there are some things all of us
are too ashamed to ever tell.

I Was the Girl Who Never Spoke

I was the girl who never spoke, the shy girl,
my head perpetually bent, my eyes averted.
The other night at the bookstore I see the new
Dick and Jane books on a display shelf, I immediately

remember how much I wanted to be a part of that Dick
and Jane world, the big white house, the huge lawn,
the upper middle class father with his cardigan and pipe.
In first grade, I loved to look at the pictures in those readers,

the books offering me a window into a world
so different from my own Italian neighborhood,
the streets of Riverside lined with two or three family
shingled houses, statues of the Virgin Mary in a grotto

in the front yards of the newer hilltop houses, no front
yard at all in the ones like ours, roses climbing trellises,
vegetable gardens crammed full of corn and tomatoes,
zucchini and peppers, fig trees, grape vines.

In first grade, I didn't know that the distance between Jane's
big white colonial and our apartment could be traced
in more than miles. I was the girl who never spoke, afraid
I'd speak in Italian instead of English, afraid, as I sometimes

am even today, that some expression common to Riverside
or some way of pronouncing a word will let everyone know
where I come from, where I belong
where I can never go.

My First Bicycle

My father picked my first bicycle, well, really my only
bicycle, out of the garbage. It was a boy's two-wheeler
that had been blue and silver, but when he brought it
home it was mostly rust. I am on 17th Street
in front of the two-family house I grew up in,
on my mother's swept sidewalk, and I climb over
the centerpiece of the bike, perch on the seat.
When I put my feet on the pedals, I imagine
I will know how to ride as though the knowledge
of bicycles was born in us, and not something

we have to learn. The neighborhood kids are gathered
around me, not because of anything I've done. Since
I am so shy I am almost invisible, but my outgoing
sister and her friends are hanging out, and I just
happen to be straddling this rusty bike
in the middle of their circle.

I place my foot on the pedals, believing that I will
be able to ride down the street. Instead, my foot flies
off the pedal and I fall onto the bar, and even after
all this time, I remember the pain of hitting that bar,
a pain so intense my eyes fill with tears, my lips tremble,
I want to scream, but am hoping no one has noticed.
I get off that bike, lift my leg over the center bar,
and balance the bike, wheeling it up the sidewalk
and down the back path

to our yard. I don't tell anyone, never try to ride
the bike again. Even now, I am ashamed
of how I must have looked, ashamed of the way
I crawled away, back to my room and books,

to the place where I felt safe, where I could imagine
riding a bicycle, my body exultant
and loose and free.

WHAT DID I WANT

What did I want as I sat in that dusty 6th grade classroom
at PS 18? Outside the windows rain, gray and bleak.
Black smoke from the factory across the street
stained the sky. Inside the room, Mrs. Richmond paced
in her high heels and tight sweaters and too bright lipstick.
She was quick to criticize, quick to turn her eyes into blue ice
that flashed and sparked. I never wanted her to look at me,
but there was no escape. The day stretched out taut, ready
to snap, and often I'd drift away from her monotone

to dream of following covered wagons across plains
to places I had never been and had little hope of going,
but in my mind, I could imagine what those places
would be like, could almost see the buffalo
as if they were roaming the streets of Paterson.

I did not know how hard it was to leave behind
the lives we were born to, the Italian neighborhood,
the cracked and broken sidewalks, the brick factories
where our parents worked, how this gray life marked us
as clearly as a scar on our faces. It was there in the way
we walked, the sound of words in our mouths.

Only in books was there a path to take us away
to a place where all things were possible,
where nothing mattered except the bright bird
in our minds who could lift up and soar away.

LITTLE HOUSE ON THE PRAIRIE

After I found the *Little House on the Prairie* books
in the Riverside Branch of the Paterson Public Library,
I read them all, my eyes moving fast across the page,
and then read them all again, fascinated by the family's
journey over mountains, across plains, admiring
the courage it took to travel that huge emptiness
to get to a place they'd never been,

while I sat in Mr. Landgraff's seventh grade at PS18
in Paterson, Mr. Landgraff who was sarcastic and mean
and handsome, in a white-haired, white-man kind of way.
Mr. Landgraff who preferred the pretty charming girls.
Mr. Landgraff who thought I was too introverted and shy.
I dreamt my way through seventh grade, imagining myself
in that covered wagon, though I hadn't left Paterson

more than twice, for in *Little House* I found the bravery
I lacked, reading all evening at home and walking to school
in the morning, sitting where Mr. Landgraff told me to sit,
crushable as a caterpillar. But after he marked off my name
in his attendance book, I floated off to Kansas and Nebraska,

sure that like Laura, I could be brave, that there was
a place out there where I could live a life as extraordinary
and risky as any I read about in books, far removed
from the chalk dust and quiet despair of seventh grade
with its green black-out shades, its picture of George
Washington, its scarred and battered desks that tried
to hold me captive.

CHANGING MY NAME

I was twelve and in seventh grade. My mother and father
called me Maria with that very Italian inflection *Mah ria.*
My brother and sister called me Mary, deciding at some
point that Mary was the American equivalent of Maria,

but in seventh grade I decided I needed to change my name,
that Maria sounded foreign, that Mary signified a life I didn't
want—plain and dull and too Catholic. It reminded me
of the Blessed Virgin. I didn't feel I could live up to her

cool blue perfection, her face, all purity and grace, floated
above her blue cape in the side altar at Blessed Sacrament
Church. That year, I remember standing in the row between
the desks talking to Camille; suddenly, I heard myself saying,

"I want everyone to call me Marie from now on," and Marie
it was that year, though as soon as I said it, the name didn't
feel right, like a sweater in a store window that looks so
exquisite, but is uncomfortable each time you wear it.

Marie was like that. Years later, I realized that I wanted to fit
in so desperately that I had given away my own true name,
Maria, the one that really fit me, the one with its Italian
sound, the one I would force

everyone to use even when they wanted to call me
Marie, the one I reclaimed the year when I discovered
that changing your life starts with accepting all the parts
of your past you were so anxious to give away.

JUDY GOT A SET OF UNDERWEAR

When I was in seventh grade, Judy got a set of underwear.
They were in a box and folded so you could see
that each one had a different day of the week printed on it.
They were made of thin rayon, a different color for each day.
I thought they were exquisite and wanted some myself
instead of the plain white cotton underwear
my mother bought for me.

Judy was baby doll pretty with her blue eyes and curly blonde
hair. We were best friends until 7th grade when Judy
discovered boys, discovered that the boys fought
with each other over her, discovered the power of her beauty
to draw them in. I was still a little girl,

did not have whatever it took to reel boys in. Judy became
best friends with Andrea, who was sexy and sophisticated
and who knew how to flirt with boys. I was left behind,
too shy to talk to boys or flirt or laugh. All the pink yellow
blue underwear in the world couldn't transform me.

PARTY GIRL

Even after all these years, I remember the red net skirt
and satin blouse my older cousin gave me for Christmas
the year I turned sixteen. The white box with Lord & Taylor
in gold was wrapped in a wide red bow, and I was so thrilled
when I opened it to find that sparkly net skirt, the smooth
satin of the blouse. "Now you can go to a party," my cousin said.
For a moment, I imagined the life she pictured for me of big teen
parties and lots of friends even though I knew I was shy and bookish
and only had a couple of friends. I asked my mother if I could
have a party, and she said yes. I invited Lois and Bill, my best
friend and her boyfriend, and Jimmy, my boyfriend,
and my friend Pat.

My mother made a cake and cookies, bought potato chips
and soda, and cleaned the apartment for hours. On the night
of the party, I called my friend Pat and by some tangle of lines
I could hear her conversation with her boyfriend. I heard him say,
"Then, don't go to her stupid party. Her mother will be there.
It will be a party for little kids," he said. "Don't go. Meet me, instead."
A little later she called and she was sorry, but wasn't feeling well
and couldn't come to my party. Then, Lois and Bill and Jimmy all called
saying they couldn't be there. My family pretended

nothing had happened. We had the potato chips, soda, cake and cookies.
I wore my party outfit, and pasted a fake smile on my face. Later, I took
the skirt and blouse off and folded them away in the lovely box, knowing
I would never wear that outfit again and that no matter what I wore,
no outfit could make me into the sophisticated party girl who should
have worn that skirt and flirted and danced all night, and not as I did,
hidden, my cat in my arms and crying into his warm fur
until I fell asleep.

Going to the Rivoli in Downtown Paterson

When we were growing up, we went to downtown Paterson
to the Rivoli theater on Main Street to see the latest movies
and the stars we loved—Rock Hudson, Doris Day,
Tab Hunter—the theater ornately carved with cherubs
and angels, elaborate moldings and glass chandeliers
and velvet curtains. That was when Paterson still thrived,
before the first shopping center opened in Elmwood Park
and then on Route 4, the Garden State Plaza and the Bergen
Mall, and people stopped taking the buses into downtown
to shop at Meyer Brothers where the elevator operators
wore white gloves and announced the goods on each floor,
before they stopped going to Quackenbush's with its curving
stair that led to the restaurant where people with money
(or more money than we had) would stop for lunch
or to Berman's for cashmere sweaters or to the Rivoli
or the Fabian to watch movies. That was in the fifties before
the wealthy people from the Eastside section moved out
to Fair Lawn or Glen Rock, before they moved to places
where they had to have a car because there was no public
transportation, before poor people started moving
into Paterson, people poorer than we were, the immigrants
who crowded into the ethnic neighborhoods like the Totowa
section or Riverside in the thirties and forties, and who by
the late fifties moved out, too, to blue collar suburbs, looking
for more space, bigger gardens, before they, too,
all bought cars and stopped walking or taking buses
and trains. On Saturdays, after school when I was a girl,
we'd take the bus downtown and we'd walk up and down
Main Street in and out of stores. We never bought anything,
but we liked wandering the aisles of Meyer Brothers,
spritzing ourselves with perfume, if we dared, and smelling
the leather purses we couldn't afford. Then we'd retreat
to the Rivoli, to the elegance of the theater, to that moment

when they'd dim the lights and the movie would flash onto
the huge screen and we'd leave behind our ordinary lives
and enter the world of the film, a place where people lived
lives that were magical and glittering, a place
where people could have whatever they desired
and never have to count the costs.

I IMAGINE MEETING ELVIS PRESLEY

I imagine meeting Elvis Presley on a street corner
in Binghamton, Elvis with his gyrating hips and his sexy
voice who blasted out of my boyfriend's car radio
when we were 17. One night while driving back
from a date he asked, "Why did you French kiss Bill?"

I said "What," the way I do now although I spent $6,000
on hearing aids that sometimes don't work. He repeated
his question and I asked, "What's French kissing?" and he
told me. "Ugh! Is that what he was doing? He danced
with me at the party and he stuck his tongue in my mouth.
It was disgusting. I thought he was crazy." I said.

Finally, Jimmy believed me and we kissed for hours parked
in the woods on William Paterson College campus, but I
never felt anything—not a single spark of electricity between
us, though he took me home to have dinner with his parents
and pretended we were "in love." He tried to tell me
that he liked going to gay clubs, asked if I wanted to go
with him. I didn't understand what he was trying to tell me.
We broke up.

Later, he wrote to me from San Francisco and said
he was gay. Some part of me had known it all along,
all those hours parked in the woods or at Garret Mountain
lookout, those hours when he kissed me until my lips were
raw and I felt nothing, nothing at all, and those interminable
dinners at his parents, me inarticulate and shy, and Jimmy
pretending that he was what his critical father wanted
him to be, and that he could live his life with me
to make his father happy, while those hours necking
must have made him feel like he was kissing someone
as appealing to him as a frog or a stone.

18

SLEEPOVER

My first sleepover was at Betty's house in Little Falls, her family's stucco and timber house on its big property. I was 19. I met Betty the first day of college and she became my best friend. My mother finally agreed to let me sleep over at Betty's house though my mother believed we were only safe when we were in our own house. Since she left Italy when she was twenty-three, she never wanted to go anywhere again. Our house was her country; she the absolute monarch, but this time, she said I could go, so I took the bus home from college with Betty and we had dinner with her family, where I had hamburgers for the first time and no one spoke except to say, "Pass the potatoes, please." No laughter. No political arguments. Her father stoic and silent. Her mother expressionless, her face frozen. Her brother eating and not looking at anyone. I was so nervous and uncomfortable I could hardly swallow. Later we sat together, Betty and I, in her bedroom and talked about school and boys and books and professors. When it was time to sleep, Betty pulled out the sofa bed in the living room and we climbed in. I felt awkward, uncomfortable. Every noise and creak in the house scared me, but finally I slept. In the middle of the night, her huge black cat jumped onto my chest and I screamed, waking up the entire house. Her mother and father ran down from upstairs, her brother appeared in the hall. I wanted to hide and I kept saying, "I'm sorry. I'm sorry." And the next morning, I couldn't look any of them in the eye. At home again, eating the food I was used to, meatballs and gravy and macaroni and *braciola,* sitting at our kitchen table, my family around me talking politics and laughing, all of us part of a group we knew we belonged to. I was grateful that Betty's family in their beautiful house was not my family, and glad to have my mother hug me to her chest where I could smell the aroma of vanilla and sugar and flour, that even today I imagine I can call my mother back from the dead and breathe her in.

19

Going to Swansea to Visit Dylan Thomas's Home

When I was nineteen, we used to go to New York City
to McSorley's or the White Horse Tavern
because that's where Dylan Thomas went to drink,
and I guess we thought if we sat in a chair
where Dylan sat, we'd pick up some of his genius.

This summer at Laugherne at Dylan's house, the last one
he lived in before he died, I saw his study, that little cabin
set on the very edge of the cliff overlooking the sea
where he wrote, his desk, his chair, his lamp, his books.
It felt sacred, a shrine to the exquisite music of his poems.

Peter Thabit Jones, the editor who drives us around
in Swansea, spoke of the Dylan Thomas industry and truly
the whole town is dedicated to Dylan, statues of him
in the square, the Dylan Thomas Theater, murals of Dylan
Thomas against which we pose, the Dylan Thomas Center
where we read with Dylan's daughter, Aeronwy. We visit
Dylan's boyhood home and it's not open to the public,
but his daughter calls the owners and they take us
on a tour. I look out his bedroom window and the window
of his parents' room, I see the vista he must have spent
hours gazing at, the one he captured in his poems, though
when he was a boy, that house at the top of the hill was
surrounded only by fields and not by the houses
that have been built up all around it. Peter takes us
to the park Dylan describes in "The Hunchback
in the Park," and to Fern Hill and I feel I have been
to these places before.

Nearly fifty years ago, I breathed in the smoky air
of the White Horse Tavern where the bartender always
asked for my ID, and I would not have imagined that

I would ever read my poems where Dylan lived and ride
in a car for days with Dylan's daughter or that I'd look out
at the Irish Sea, and see what he showed the world
in his poems, so that looking at the stretch of coast,
I am certain I know it, as if I had grown up there myself
and not in a Paterson ghetto with no view of the sea wall
or of the birds that rise and dip above us.

LIES WE TELL OURSELVES

In the picture I am twenty years old, my eyes look enormous
in my thin face, my hair springs wildly off my head, thick
and shiny, my face seems lit by a rose-colored spotlight.
I am excited and happy and then, as now, everything shows
in my face. At the college dance, I am sitting at a round table,
between Chuck and Bob. They both have their arms around
me and their faces close to mine. We are all smiling. Chuck is
my first lover, though when I met him at the Literary Club, I
didn't like him. He wasn't one of the blond, blue-eyed boys I
always fell for because they made me feel American, helped
me erase everything in myself I hated, but he persisted,
asked me out again and again, until I finally said yes. It took
him six months to get me past my Catholic guilt, my fear
of undressing and of sex, and into bed, though actually we
made love, as we called it then, mostly in cars. Sometimes
he'd sneak me into his house and we'd make love in his
bedroom that still looked like a boy's room. The picture
catches me looking at Bob and Bob looking at me, though
I should have been looking that way at Chuck. Bob told me
I had eyes as deep as the Indian Ocean, and came with us
on our dates because his girl was away at college. The three
of us would sit together at the movies or college dances
or at McSorley's or the Blue Note or Greenwich Village, the three
of us riding in the front seat of Chuck's car, Bob half in love
with me and I half in love with him, though it was Chuck
who made love to me in any hidden place he could find.
And I'm sure he told Bob everything, but I admit I loved sex
better than I loved Chuck.

When the Factory Whistle Blows

When the factory whistles used to blow, the whole town
was called to start their day and end it. The summer
I worked at Marcal Paper Factory, I had to be at my work
station at 7 a.m. exactly; that's when they'd start the conveyor
belt. We packed boxes of Christmas wrapping paper, slipping
each pattern out of the shelves above the belt and stacking
them, so they could be sealed in cellophane wrap. The woman
on the front end of the conveyer was used to piecework,
having worked in a factory all her life. I had to run up
and down the line to keep up. The next day, they raised
the speed of the machine, and I told the woman
to slow down. She looked at me as though I were a slug,
her face flat and cold. "Come on, college girl," she said.
"Keep up." At 12, the whistle would sound for lunch
and we'd rush across the factory to the box room
where we ate lunch we brought in paper bags
from home. We sat on boxes, our sandwiches in wax paper
on our laps. We had twenty minutes for lunch and we had
to allow time to get back to the belt. By 3:30, when the closing
bell sounded, I couldn't wait to climb back into my father's
car to go home. Something about this place,
the dust, the lack of light, seemed to drain the life from
the people who worked there. I kept having nightmares
about being stuck there for the rest of my life, as my parents
were stuck in their separate factories, though they never
complained. Two of the workers hid behind one
of the machines to make love during lunch. They were
married to other people. One day, the boss said we're
moving you to the toilet paper machine and he showed me
how to operate it. I had to place my hand inside to pull out
each roll of paper after the sharp blade had sliced it off. I was
certain that one day I wasn't going to be fast enough
and the blade was going to slice off my hand.

Only after I left in late August, and was walking out
of the red brick fortress, did I feel sad for the people
who remained, while I escaped into my other life of books
and teachers and friends and parties and out of the gray
dust that covered everything, away from the factory whistles
that punctuated their lives.

THE MOST DANGEROUS THING I EVER DID

At Eastside High School, most of the Jewish
girls had their noses done, all of us wanting to erase
any hint of ethnicity or race. I envied those girls, so bright
and competent, those girls who could afford to change
their noses into proper American noses and not the ethnic
noses we were born wearing. As soon as I started to work
after college, I paid for a Master's degree and when I got
my first college teaching job, I decided I was going to have my
nose done. I made an appointment with a plastic surgeon, told
him what I wanted, and he told me what day to report
to the hospital and I signed myself in. I was terrified that
my parents would find out and kill me, but I went through
with it anyway. On the operating table, I heard the doctor say,
"We're going to give her a perfect nose," and then, I swear, I heard
him break the bone in my nose. When I woke up I had bandages
over my nose and two enormous black eyes. I was in the hospital
two days and then I called home and told my mother
that I had fallen on the road and hit the curb in the college town,
where the conference was held and where I had never been.
As with all lies, my story was perhaps a little too elaborate.
I think my mother guessed, but my father would have killed me,
so she didn't tell him anything. Instead, she nursed me back
to health, bringing me chicken soup, toast and tea. When my cousin
came to visit, she said, "Oh, your nose looks the same to me." I knew
she was saying it to make me feel that my hooked nose had not changed
at all, but I was happy to be rid of it, to have become American
or so I thought. Years later, I am ashamed of my willingness to erase
that nose, so large and unmistakable, for this ordinary, inoffensive
nose, this American nose, my hooked nose, always there
on the inside, always Italian, always mine.

How I Met You

Why is it when I think of you I think first of your coming into
Dick's white colonial house in River Edge, you with your blond
crew cut, you with eyes deep as Blue Willow china, you
with your wide shoulders, you playing your guitar, singing
"Black, Black Is the Color of My True Love's Hair." I swear
everyone else in that living room disappeared as soon as you
started to sing and I, who did not believe in love at first sight,
was overcome with longing, loved you as passionately that day
as I would love you for the rest of our lives together, though
I was ashamed that Dick, your best friend, the one who had invited
me to his house for dinner and invited you over to meet me, the boy
I'd been dating for two months no longer existed for me, and though
I was sorry, though I tried to make it up to him by introducing him
to my friends, until on the third try at matchmaking he met the friend
he married 43 years ago, I didn't care, couldn't stop myself from loving
you, I wanted only to reach out and touch the high cheekbones
of your face. At your funeral, our daughter created a collage of pictures
of you. In one, your arm is around Dick's shoulders in that very male 1950s
way, and Dick looks at the picture and says, as he has said each time he's
seen us over the years, "There's the man who stole my girl." I turn away,
tears filling my eyes, wishing I could bring you back the way you were all
those years ago, so young, so strong, so perfect for me that we were
like two pieces of a magnetic puzzle that fit together with a satisfying click,
you still able to swim and ride your bike and climb hills and not, of course,
broken as you were by the time you died. I smile when I think of you
in Dick's living room forty-seven years ago, lamplight shining on your hair,
and the way I knew in that moment that you were the man I'd marry,
and nothing else mattered then or now.

LOOKING BACK THAT YEAR, EVERYTHING SEEMED POSSIBLE

... we were young, in love, the children still babies really,
Jennifer not even two, John four. We packed up the car
with the things we thought we'd need until the moving
truck got to Kansas City. Before we left, I went
to the bank with your friend, Richard. On the way back,
he said, "Please don't leave. Stay here with me. Please."
And he kissed me. I struggled out of his arms,
said, "I have to go," feeling stupid that I didn't realize
how he felt, embarrassed for us both and frightened,
you waiting for us, and I, suddenly terrified
at leaving New Jersey and my family, riding in this car
with Richard who wanted me to leave you. Did he want
the children, too? I almost laughed at the thought. I never
told you. When we said goodbye, Richard hugged me
and shook your hand in that semi-distant way men do.

We set off in our sedate brown Plymouth on the adventure
of our lives, off to a state we'd never seen, that was far
enough away it was almost another country, "Kansas City,"
we said, as though we were going to Paris or Rome.
The children played in the back seat on those long drives
between motels. You sang folk songs and led us on sing fests,
and I played games with the children to keep them
entertained. How fortunate we were, our lives stretching
like a glittering belt before us. You held my hand and I kept
my hand on your knee. We were in love. How could we
lose? Looking back that year, everything seemed possible.
The Missouri sky, deep and wide, a black velvet tent above
our heads. So blessed we were, so blessed that we could not
see what lay just around the curve ahead, so blessed that we
did not know how much we had yet to learn, how vulnerable
we are, how all the love in the world cannot protect us.

In that car, riding toward our future, we are so certain we have only to reach out our hands and grab everything we want and are sure we deserve.

WHO COULD KNOW WHAT WOULD HAPPEN, WE WERE YOUNG

...each of us twenty-nine years old, Jennifer two,
John four. We lived in that big white stone house

with the pillars that rose right up to the roof and the wide
veranda at 5711 Oak Street, Kansas City, Missouri. You rode
your bike to the university where you taught. I traded

babysitting with a friend so I could go to the university
to teach. It was the late sixties. We had friends who lived
in a commune. We had a consciousness-raising group.

We called ourselves feminists, but I was a feminist who never
burned my bra; anti-war, though I didn't have the courage to
refuse to pay my taxes as my friend did so that the government

impounded her car. Mostly, I was as shy as I had been as a child,
caught up in loving my husband and children, enjoying my big
house that we bought because I loved the sun pouring through

the large windows, loved the breakfast room off the kitchen
where we ate most of our meals, loved the big rooms
and the back stairway and all the things I had wanted

since I was a child growing up in that small tenement
apartment in Paterson, New Jersey. I have images
in my head of that time, you reading to the children

from the *Wizard of Oz* books, me playing games with them,
all of us certain that we were exactly where we were supposed
to be, blessed with the belief that our happiness

was deserved and would never be broken. How could we
know that you would get sick when you were only forty-five,
that Jennifer, the curly-haired two year old who sat

in the rocking chair on the front porch, would marry a man
who would break her heart and we would all sit together
in our family room while she cried through so many sodden

hours, how could we know that the blessings we were sure
we deserved and took for granted in that sun-lit house
on Oak Street, would be snatched from us and we'd have

to learn all the secrets of making do, those secrets our mothers
tried to teach us, though we wouldn't listen to them.

WHAT IS IT I LOVE WHEN I LOVE YOU?

Is it the memory of you as a young man, the one
I can never quite erase from my head. You lit up
as though a spotlight were trained on you.

You on the corner near NYU graduate school, you calling
me, and I, knowing your voice, turning to you, your face so
clean cut, so blond, so American. I imagine that when you
move toward me it is like a scene of lovers moving toward
one another in a movie.

What is it I love when I love you? Is it you as a young father
holding the children's hands and walking with them
to the playground or on the campground road, you
holding my hand as we sat around the fire at night
after the children were asleep in the tent near us?

What is it I love when I love you? Is it the way you lean
your bent head against my breast, put your trembling arms
around me, even now, when this disease is paring away
at you until your legs are so weak they can't hold you up?
Is it the way you say I'm so lucky to have you and the way
it's always been, the way you pull me toward you as though
we were attached to one another by a silken cord
and it is this I love when I love you.

SOMETIMES I FEEL AS THOUGH I'M BACK IN SIXTH GRADE

Remember the nasty girls, their petty meanness,
the way they couldn't see anyone else's point
of view but their own,

remember exactly that feeling of being all
wrong, elbows, knees, too knobby and loose,
hair too thick and curly and wild,
a face too long and sad.

Remember clearly that feeling of being attacked
when my friend uses words as bullets
to destroy everything I've become, her eyes
as flat and mean and jealous as those girls
at twelve who couldn't wait to find
the vulnerable center of anyone too shy
and weak to fight back.

Remember that moment years ago, as we rode
through Riverside in your car, a year after
we were married, arguing so wildly that you ran
the red light and the cop stopped us and gave
you a ticket. "Don't fight while you're driving,"
he said, my face still shiny with tears. I needed
you too much then and when you said it: "Find
something else to do besides me," a door inside
me slammed shut and now, 40 years later, even
though I always loved you more than you wanted,
more than anybody should, the hours of our life
together, this illness that has changed what we are,
the life I have built for myself away from you
where I can leave behind that girl who thought
no one loved her.

Now, it is you who need me more than I need
you, who can't wait to know exactly what time I will
walk in the door, you who want to touch my hair.

I turn into those twelve year olds I hated. What
meanness is it in me that would run away from your
muscles wasted by this disease, the way your neck
is a bent stalk that cannot hold your head up,
your hands so weak they can't hold a pen to write
your name, that would almost say, "Hah, what does it feel
like now," even as your frailty rips at my heart. I hold you,
and say, "Don't be afraid. I'm here. I'm here."
"Don't leave me," you say. "What
would I do without you?"

I CHOOSE NOT TO REMEMBER

Looking back, I paint my memories in pastel water colors,
the edges blurred, all rough patches smoothed out.
I choose not to remember the violent arguments we had,
the way you shoved me out of your way
when I said something you didn't like, the times
you nearly pushed me down the stairs.
I choose not to remember how your rage
was a bomb always ready to go off,
even when we were on vacation in Montreal,
and you yelled and I cried, cursing you under my breath
until I fell into a 3 a.m. sleep in a dingy motel room,
even when we were riding in a car
with the children and you got lost and refused
to stop at a gas station for directions
and shouted at me instead.

Sometimes, I wonder how much our children remember
of those years we howled at each other, the years
when it looked as if this marriage were cracking apart.
I never ask them, afraid of what they heard.
It's easier not to remember the way things really were,
me always making excuses for you,
you always able to get me back, sex the way
we made up until we both pretended only that mattered
and not the argument that went before.
It's easier not to remember or how could I go on now
that you are so frail and defenseless, how could I help you
into your wheelchair or button your shirt or snap on your bib,
how could I translate your slurred speech for others
or coordinate the string of people I hire to help you
when I'm not there?

I try to explain to my daughter that sound, loud and final
as Big Ben, that happened in my head when I first saw you, the
way you, the man I loved, could create in me a fury equal to
that love. I can only survive by lying to myself about what
would have happened if I had gotten sick, if I were the one who
needed help, though you have chosen to forget the perilous
course of our marriage, and instead you buy me flowers now,
sentimental cards, hold my hand. I choose to believe you
would love me, even if I were sick and bedridden and needed
you to brush away my tears.

ON SUMMER EVENINGS

On summer evenings, we'd sit on my sister's front porch
on Oak Place and talk and laugh and tell stories.
My sister, outgoing and vivacious, loved to laugh.
The street was lined with huge oaks. The house was built
on what once had been a park and the trees were huge
and leaned over the street forming an archway of thick
summer leaves. I was teaching then, but in the summer
I didn't have papers to grade and lessons to plan, so after
supper Dennis and I would walk across the street to sit
with Laura and her husband and assorted friends.
We could sit in the dark for hours, our children
playing together in the street or inside

the house. That was before my sister got really sick,
before the rheumatoid arthritis twisted her hands and feet,
before she was ashamed of what the arthritis had done to her.
We sat on her wide front porch, screened in so we didn't have
to battle mosquitoes, and to us, time was a lake, smooth
and unruffled, that we could sail on forever. We couldn't imagine
a time when these nights on Laura's front porch would seem
magical, so blessed we were, so unaware.

I AM HERE IN THE PATHMARK AMONG THE CHEESES

I am here in the Pathmark among the cheeses
when I remember learning how to dance, my older sister,
playing the man, leading me around the dining room
in the 19th Street apartment, one/two/three/four,
one/two/three/four. The music, violins and horns,
Frank Sinatra singing, my body stiff and awkward,
my sister pushing, tugging, trying to teach me
a rhythm that was born in her bones, "Loosen up,"
she kept saying, "Loosen up," and I tried but my body refused
to be anything but shy and terrified. My sister always loved
to dance, her Marilyn Monroe body, her slender, perfectly
formed legs and feet, her high heels, her full, sexy lips,
painted with Fire and Ice lipstick, her straight teeth.

I am here in the Pathmark assaulted by the memory
of the night we sat together at my sister's house eating
cheese and crackers and drinking highballs and talking, how
those nights gradually thinned out and finally disappeared
after my sister, diagnosed at thirty with rheumatoid arthritis,
got gradually worse and worse, until by forty-five, when her
hands and feet were so obviously deformed, she stopped
wanting to be social, to have people see her though she'd
always been gregarious and outgoing.

Her illness made her ashamed and finally she could no longer
dance, her feet so twisted the bones poked through the skin.
I would sit in her den, holding her hand, thinking of us as
young girls, my sister with her raging energy, her electric
smile, teaching me how to dance, her girlfriends coming to
the apartment where they danced the jitterbug and rhumba
while I watched, my sister always happy to be moving,
her body sexy and alive.

MY DAUGHTER'S YEARBOOK FROM GEORGETOWN

Yesterday, I walked into my daughter's room, the room she
grew up in, the room she comes back to now when she visits me,
and I noticed my daughter's yearbook on top
of the bookshelf. She was the editor. My daughter is sitting
on her bed holding her laptop and working on a book. She
notices me noticing the yearbook and she says, "What was I
thinking? My hair, my clothes are all wrong, that eighties
look. When I got to Georgetown," she says, "I was so tacky."
I protest. She says, "Look at my hair. All these upper middle
class people, and there I am with my too big hair, my clothes
not preppy enough and not from the right stores, even
the way I said 'Hore thorne,' instead of Hawthorne. It's so
embarrassing when I think of it." "Remember grandma saw
your yearbook, how she kept touching the pages saying, 'How
beautiful, how beautiful,' looking at all those healthy, smiling
students with their straight teeth and their shining skin.
'Only in America,' grandma said, before she pats the book
and gets up to serve dinner." My daughter has heard
this all before, nothing will convince her. "I was tacky,"
she says, and I think of her getting ready for her wedding
in this room, how incredibly stunning she was in that gown
and veil, how happy, and now ten years since her divorce,
the light that used to shine in her face has dimmed, she looks
in the mirror and sees something flawed and I want only
to find the words that will make her see herself as beautiful,
make her see the future, not as huge gray clouds moving
toward her, but instead as a wide road opening outward
to a vista wide as the sea.

THE CIGAR FACTORIES IN YUBA CITY, FLORIDA

In 1860, Yuba City imported Cuban and Italian
immigrants to work in the cigar factories.
The Cubans learned Italian; the Italians learned
Spanish. With no social security or health insurance,
groups banded together to form Mutual Benefit Societies
to provide money for members who got sick
and for the widows and children of people who died.
They put money together to pay a "reader,"
someone who would sit in front of the workers
and read books to them to help time pass
and keep them entertained. Their days were long,
no time for formal schooling but they listened
to classic books in Spanish and Italian until the bosses,
in the 1920s, banned the reader from the factories.

My parents, too, were Italian immigrants who came
to Paterson to work in factories; they, too, belonged
to a Mutual Benefit Society that provided
what the factory owners and government did not,
help for the sick and widows and children, but by 1930,
life in the factories was all about efficiency, and keeping
the workers in line. Once when I was seventeen,
I visited the factory where my mother worked.
It was on the second floor up a flight of narrow,
rickety stairs, and when I opened the door,
the noise of sewing machines slapped my face.
I searched for my mother in the close-packed row
of women bent over their sewing. The floor manager
picked up one of the pieces my mother had finished,
screamed, "You call this sewing?" and threw the coat
on the floor. The tables were lit by bare light bulbs,
dangling down on cords. I had never seen the place
where my mother worked. She thought we should be

protected from all that was ugly and mean
in the grown-up world. "Children should be children,"
she'd say. "They'll learn trouble soon enough.
We don't need to tell them about it." She did not answer
the floor walker. Instead she bent her head over her sewing,
but not before I saw the shame in her face.

My Mother's Mulberry Trees

In her garden, my mother planted a mulberry tree.
She'd let it grow for eight years, its bark smooth
to the touch, then she'd chop it down and start again.
In between, it provided shade for her tiny walk and patio.
In the rest of her garden, she planted tomatoes, peppers,
basil, oregano, rosemary, cucumber, lettuce, string beans,
corn and a line of sunflowers that raised their faces
to the cauldron of the sun. My mother never stopped
working. My mother was so full of energy it was as though
she were attached to high voltage wire. My mother
recreated the farm she left behind when she was a girl
on that mountain in Italy, the plants startlingly green
and alive. In the three months it took her to die, Jennifer,
my daughter, and I picked tomatoes, peppers, corn,
and zucchini and carried the baskets into her bedroom
so she could see them. Jennifer and I could barely keep up
with the harvest as though the garden wanted to give her
one last crop, enormous and perfect, so that she could place
the basil and mint and tomatoes to her nose
and draw the fragrance in.

My Mother Worked So Hard

When I was growing up we lived in a two-family house
on 17th Street in Paterson, NJ. The kitchen was the largest
room in the house with its black cast iron coal stove
that heated the room, one door for the coal and another
for the oven and four burners, and in front of the stove
was the kitchen table covered with oilcloth and the dangling
light fixture overhead and the icebox cooled by ice
that the ice man delivered two times a week, and the milk
that was in glass bottles and was brought to the door by the milkman
from Lakeview Dairy who also delivered butter in a stone
crock. On the other side of the kitchen, my mother's padded
rocker. Off the kitchen, two bedrooms—room enough
for a three-quarter bed and a small bureau. The beds
were made of metal, not brass, but some base metal,
utilitarian, plain, almost ugly on purpose. My mother tried
to make the apartment as beautiful as no money would
allow—embroidered dresser scarves she brought from Italy
and 5 and 10 cent knick knacks she bought with hoarded
pennies. Years later when she was dying, her bedroom, still
small, held her burnished maple bed and a large dresser
with a full-sized mirror. On the dresser, a statue
of the Blessed Virgin, blue gowned and lovely, and a votive
candle and a bouquet of silk flowers. Over the bed post
a rosary; my mother said her prayers each night, counting off
the beads. Long after we had grown up, my mother would go
to garage sales and buy expensive knick knacks and oil
paintings, all the lovely things she wanted but couldn't afford
during those Paterson tenement years, and then she died.
The estate sale people came into her neat house and sold off
all her things, strangers carted off her bed and mirror,
the statue of the Blessed Virgin, the silk flowers, the old
paintings, until the house was empty of everything
she tried to do to make it a home.

AT THE BREAKFAST TABLE

This morning at the breakfast table I talk about you,
describe how you always criticized me, how I'd walk in your
back door, and you'd say, "Why don't you do something
with your hair or that dress doesn't look right, or are you gaining
weight?" and when I complained, you said, "But if I don't tell you,
who will? Do you think your friends care about you? Do you
think they'll try to help you?" You did try to stop yourself
when I explained how your words hurt, tried to keep yourself
from saying anything, though I'd see you studying me when
I came in the door, but you'd say, "Come in, come in. I don't
have anything to give you." Then you'd open the 1950s Kelvinator
and pull dish after dish, *braciole*, pasta, homemade macaroni, fish,
roasted chicken, salad. "What do you want," you'd say and then you'd
decide for me, serve me a meal anytime of day and after we'd eaten,
you'd make espresso in the stainless steel pot, the *machinate* you called it,
pour it into those little cups with their little saucers and their small spoons,
and we'd sit together and you'd take my hand. Even with all your criticism,
even with all the times you said don't tell my secrets in your poems, I always
knew you would come to me the moment I needed you, take care of me
the way no one else would. I tell the people at the table the story of you
when you looked at Jennifer's Georgetown yearbook and you turned to me
and said, "You know, I was so proud of you when you graduated from college."
I asked why you waited twenty-five years to tell me and you said,
"Oh, I didn't want to bring bad luck on you." Talking about you in this sunlit
room, though you died twenty years ago, I say, "I miss my mother," and suddenly
my eyes fill with tears, I imagine you are with me once again, you, stroking my
hand, you, still looking at me, with love in your eyes, you whom I think of every
day, wishing I could drive to your home and sit at your kitchen table, and we
could have espresso together and you could hold me while I cry.

CONJURING UP MY MOTHER

Why this morning, twenty years after my mother died,
do I conjure her up in her basement kitchen, clear
as if I had seen her yesterday? Watch her lift the roasting
pan out of the oven, the chicken browned and sizzling,
the oven-roasted potatoes, sliced and quartered, brown
and gold. Watch her pull out the stuffed artichokes, dark
green leaves holding homemade breadcrumbs that have formed
a crust while the artichokes cooked. She places the food carefully
as an artist on serving platters in the basement dining room
where 16 of us sit around three tables placed end to end
to form a long row. The chicken and artichokes are the third
course she has served this Sunday, as she does each Sunday, her
children and grandchildren laughing and talking, take for granted
the aroma of tomato sauce and homemade ravioli, meatballs, bowls
of olives and walnuts, huge salads from her garden, the entire meal
ending with her special lemon cake and bowls of fruit and cookies
and espresso. Such bounty presented to us each week as though it
would go on forever, my mother happy to be cooking for hours before
we arrived from our morning coffee and *NY Times* and sleeping in, happy
to see us all together at her table, the way we came to believe we deserved
to be served, came to believe she would always be there. Even now, I imagine
I can see the crispy skin of that chicken, long since eaten, the crusty potatoes,
the artichoke leaves, the bread stuffing, that I could drive to her house
and she'd be waiting for me, and not as I do now, each day, all the voices
that surrounded me vanished, only this memory to comfort me in my empty
house where too often, I eat alone.

MY FATHER WORKED THE THIRD SHIFT

My father worked the third shift for ten years before
he retired from a rubber factory. He'd leave the plant
at 7 a.m. and drive his old clunker of a Chevy from Paterson
to Hawthorne, stopping on the way home on Sunday mornings
to buy crumb buns, because he knew we liked them.

Once a friend told him he could get him a better job,
and he left his job and tried out the new one, but he only
lasted a week before he realized he couldn't drag
that paralyzed leg through the heavy work of lifting
200 pound rolls of silk. When he went to ask
for his old job back, the boss said, "Sorry,

but I will only take you back if it is as though you never worked
here before—start at a lower wage, no vacation or sick days.
No pension." My father agreed because he had no choice.
He went back to watching the gauges on steam boilers
to make sure they didn't explode. My mother was furious.

My father never carried a grudge. It wasn't in him.
He wasn't even angry at his father who deserted his family—my
grandmother and seven children—and went to Argentina
and never came back. "Oh well," he said, right before he died
at 92, "we don't know what made him do that. Maybe he had

a good reason." Once my father was talking about the past
on one of the nights that I went over to his house to sit
with him after my mother died, and he told me about the time
he was hurt on the job when a window fell on his back
and he ended up in the hospital. The boss came to see him

and he was so thrilled that the boss took time out to visit him,
but the boss had come to fire him for getting hurt on the job.

My father was disappointed and his feelings were hurt,
but then he said, "Oh well, what can you do? It's so long ago.
It doesn't matter anymore."

There Is Only This Moment

The photo my brother-in-law sent me is from 1922.
My mother-in-law is a teenager, and is wearing
gym clothes made of a soft white material, fine cotton,
the outfit almost beautiful. My mother-in-law looks
incredibly young and energetic. She loved sports,
went on to teach physical education at St. Joseph's College
in Brooklyn, but that was several years later. In this photo,
she is just a kid with buck teeth and a broad grin. There is only
this moment, my mother-in-law surrounded by her teammates.
She cannot know what will happen later in her life, the way
she'll move in with me after her heart attack when she
couldn't live alone and had no choice, the way Alzheimer's
took over her mind until she, who had always read at least
one mystery novel a day, forgot how to read. I'd find her sitting
with a book in her hands and staring off into the distance,
the book upside down, the pages never turned. Soon she started
imagining people were coming out of the TV to get us or that
our neighbor, the one with two young children, wanted
to murder us or that moving men were coming to take all
the furniture. Her eyes full of fury, she'd sit in her rocker
and rock violently back and forth until she made holes in the walls.
My mother-in-law, who went to college in 1924 when so few women
went to college, had become a person I no longer recognized.
I hold this picture in my hand, see her in her white costume, see
her caught at the moment in her life when all things must have
seemed possible, life as an apple, red, perfect, not bruised.
She has only to reach out her hand.

RIDING A HARLEY WITH JAMES DEAN

Some days I imagine I can take off into
another life, riding a Harley with James Dean,
his handsome doomed face, his black leather
jacket, the muscles in his legs, long and hard,

imagine that in this other life I would have
the courage to climb up behind him on that
Harley, put my arm around him and hang on,
the speed of that ride and the road sliding by

under us exhilarating, leaving behind all
that ties me to my ordinary life, the one I run
from, one project leading to the next so I won't
have to confront the sharp-edges of the world

inside my Oak Place house, the world where
each day you lose more of what you once were,
your legs refusing to move, your voice unable
to be heard, the world where James Dean

and the Harley are only a celluloid fantasy
in Technicolor and not my black and white life
with its acrid odor of medicine and loss.

Why Is It When I Think of You

I think first of you so many years ago on the corner at NYU,
your hair glowing in the street light, your high cheekbones,
your incredible gray eyes, you calling my name. If I close
my eyes I can still see you, see the way I turned toward you,
see the way I loved you, so totally that everyone in that
Greenwich Village street disappeared. You are gone now
for more than a year and this weekend, when I walk
into the hotel my friend asks: "Is it strange not to have
to call Dennis?" and I think of all the years of your illness
when I ran away to keep from knowing the future that
was rushing toward us, my busyness a shield and a curtain,
the man I loved and married forty-five years ago, gradually
pared away until he became the person in a diaper,
the person whose legs no longer worked, the person who
needed to be fed, the person who needed two caretakers
around the clock, the person who imagined he was Peter Pan
and who forgot how to put on his pants.

"I love you," I said on the phone, even as I worked harder
and harder so I wouldn't have time to know that you could not
win against this disease, that no matter how much I held onto
your hand I could not keep you with me or turn you back into
that handsome young man at NYU or get back all those years
in between when we traveled together to Italy and France
and England and Spain and Portugal or the camping trips
throughout the southwest and all those evenings at the plays
and movies and museums we loved, could not get you back
the way you were, and instead you became the burden
I could no longer carry, the person in my mirror, selfish
and ugly, wanting only to clean out the house of the ladies
who take care of you, the smell of medicine and the equipment
you needed, hospital bed, electric wheelchairs, walkers, hoya lifts,
the house too full of everything I could not stand to know,

and even you whom I loved so long, I am ashamed that I wanted
you gone, so today I would ask you to forgive me,
if I could, ask you to forgive my impatience, my desire
to live only for myself alone.

How Complicated Life Is

1.
This evening, we talk about a drug which chemists
developed to halt the death of the cells
in your brain. I have lost hope in all these new
medicines. Nothing works, nothing makes this disease stop
its progress. I have loved you since I was a young woman.

Lately, I can feel my heart shutting down, each new loss
you suffer closing my heart against you. Our lives have become
a minefield I cross each day, landmines waiting to explode
if I step in just the wrong place.

2.
When I am invited to read my poems in China you say,
"Don't go. You could get hurt. It's so far away.
I am afraid of what will happen if you die."

"Remember when John was born and the doctors
told you to go home, that he wouldn't be born yet,
and you never came back until hours after he was born?"

"I was sleeping," you said, and I am crazily furious
 over something that happened thirty-eight years ago.
"I am not selfish like that anymore," you say, your voice
shaking, and I am ashamed of remembering every time
you were not there when I needed you, of not remembering

the times when you were there, believing in my most secret
heart that if I had gotten sick, as you are sick, you would have
left me, though that is a secret I try to keep even from myself.
I look for an excuse for going to China, for doing what I want

to do rather than thinking of you, caught more and more
in your electric wheelchair. In my mind I imagine China—all
red and gold and shiny, and then I picture you, so broken
and afraid. Sitting beside you, holding your hand,
all the words I can never speak, stuck
in my mouth like a stone.

THE LADIES TAKE DENNIS TO THE MALL

I call home last night. Claudia and Althea tell me
they hired a car and took Dennis grocery
shopping and to the mall. They are thrilled.
Imagine my intellectual husband who was never one
for malls or grocery stores being pushed around
stores by these exuberant ladies. I wonder, if he
is so desperate to get out of the house that even
something he wouldn't have wanted to do
twenty years ago seems enchanting to him now.
Dennis is having his supper, they tell me. He's not
so sleepy anymore, but he's hard to understand.
They hand him the phone and he tries to talk
but he sounds like a stroke victim, and I who felt
happy for a moment that he had an excursion,
am overcome by loss. "I'm thinking about you,"
I say, but I'm not sure he understands. "I'll be home
soon." He has trouble forming words, though
he's trying to tell me something. I think it's
"I love you."

POEM ON OUR 45TH ANNIVERSARY

I watch you in the dentist's chair, the chair we struggled
to get you into, Yvonne, the aide, the nurses, and I lifting
you from the wheelchair into the chair where your head
is bent sideways and unable to relax so it is caught
in an awkward position. We try to prop up your head
with a pillow and a blanket. It doesn't work. The doctor
tells us that's dystonia. There is nothing to be done.
You who have always taken such good care of your teeth,
those fat strong teeth that crunched into apples for so
many years have broken off at the gum line now
because the medicine ate away at them until they
were hollow. The dentist puts an IV in your arm
and gradually your eyes close and you sleep.
"You can leave now," the dentist says. "We'll call you
when we're finished." Yvonne goes out into the hall
and starts crying. I feel like crying too. You were
so handsome as a young man, with your blond hair,
your blue/grey eyes, your high cheekbones, those straight,
strong teeth. Every year, one more thing is taken
from you, until you have to be fed and changed, your legs
unable to move so you're forced to use a wheelchair
and to be helped from the chair into the car,
and now this. When they call me, you are drowsy
and blood stains your face and your jeans and shirt.
Gauze is crammed into your mouth. I hold your hand
or try to, but your hand is formed into a claw so you can't
hold on. All those years ago when I walked down the aisle
at St. Anthony's Church toward you, my whole body
trembling, I could not have imagined a day when you'd be
so broken, nor did I know then how brave you are, the way
you don't complain, the way you say, "I'm not afraid," the
way you say, "I don't need the pain killer, it doesn't hurt that
much," the way you carry this illness like a sack on your back,

and though it is filled with bricks, you act as if it is light as air.
"I read an article on stem cells," you tell me. "Maybe
I'll survive long enough so they can cure me."

IN THE MONTHS IT TOOK YOU TO DIE

In the months it took you to die, I ran around
to readings and teaching, driving up Rte. 17 West
toward Binghamton to get away from the smell
of urine and medicine that filled our house,
to get away from your eyes that followed me
wherever I went and no matter how far, wanting
to get you back the way you were before this disease
began its unrelenting assault, twenty-five years of it
until it took so much of the man I loved for forty-six
years, so much that I had to force myself to look at you
and know the end of this story.

When we were young, on Saturday mornings, you'd do
odd jobs around the house, sipping a glass of wine
and relaxing, working with your hands, a rest from the life
of the mind you lived all week and by afternoon, happy
and slightly crocked, the children playing outside
or in the basement, you'd call me from wherever I was,
chasing dust balls under dressers and beds, your voice
like honey and you'd pull me into the downstairs bath
and I'd object that the children would hear, but your hands
made me shiver and, the good little Italian girl, would be
transformed like the frog who turned into a prince in fairy
tales, and I'd be a woman so besotted with you that you
could talk me into making love anywhere, even standing up.
or lying down in the bathroom, which luckily I had just
cleaned, even when I was afraid the children would hear,
even when I was embarrassed at my own lust, and now,

standing next to your hospital bed, you in your diaper
that is too big, even though it's the smallest size,
you with your legs too weak to hold you, I remember
how much I loved your body, how muscular your legs

and back, how all the prayers in the world cannot
bring you back the way you were then, so alive,
so unaware of what waited for us in the years ahead.

Sooner or Later We Face the Dark

Driving eighty miles an hour down Route 80 in Pennsylvania,
I fall asleep at the wheel,

and only wake up because I am bouncing up and down
on the grassy median heading straight

for a highway sign, I snap out of it and turn the wheel
without looking because my side view

mirror is not adjusted and I didn't know whether I was
heading straight for a car or truck

when I bounce back onto the highway, though I did see
a tractor trailer veer over to the right to avoid

hitting me. The rest of the way back to Binghamton,
I drive, both my hands clutching the wheel, my back

straight, concentrating on staying awake long enough
to reach my apartment. Sooner or later we face

the dark and yesterday I did, realizing that I escaped
death twice, once on that grassy median and once

when I lurched back onto the highway. I could be dead,
and then who would take care

of my husband and who would help my daughter? Looking
back, I remember all the narrow

escapes I've had—the time I stopped breathing
when they gave me an antibiotic I was allergic

to after surgery—the only person in history to spend
fourteen days in a hospital after gallbladder surgery

or the time I had my tonsils out and I didn't wake up
for two days or the time I had a D&C and they couldn't stop

the bleeding despite yards of cotton packing
and hormone shots and thirty days in bed. But each

time, no matter how fine the line between me
and death, the line has been there, thin and elastic,

snapping me back into life with the force of a slingshot,
so for days after I am dizzy

and disoriented, repeating to myself,
I'm a lucky woman. I'm a lucky woman.

DRIVING IN THE CATSKILLS

1.
Today, the mountain stream curves
through the valley. Above it, the mountains soften
into spring and the sun turns the stream silver.
After this long winter, after weeks of snow and rain,
I'm drawn to this tender beauty. I imagine
the flowers just below the surface
of the earth ready to burst
into bloom.

2.
It's mid-April and after two weeks of sunshine and warm
weather, today it turns bleak and cold. I drive down
Route 17 west toward Binghamton, and even the mountains
and trees don't look soft with spring.

On campus the wind whirls and howls around the buildings,
and the windows of this corner room, and the young people
and their parents rush across campus, the wind whipping
at their too-light clothes. The mother in her silk shirt
gives her son a coat and shoves her own way indoors.
My mood slides lower into grayness and even the poems
that blossom in this room, the faces of these students
who surround me, cannot lift the veil of sorrow
through which I cannot move.

3.
Surrounded by the soft curves of the Catskills,
Route 17 west unrolls like a belt in front of my car.
Mid-October, the trees just starting to turn, some pale
yellow, some just slightly faded. In between, the evergreens
deep green feathers sweep the sky. All those colors of gray,
clouds upon clouds, some dark as smoke. What a blessing
this beauty is, healing as salve on my skin.

WHAT PROTECTS US

In the airport screening line, the officer says, "What do you
have on?" Something shows up on the machine and she points
to my breast. I mumble and can't find the right words
to explain. Can I say that I'm a university professor and a poet,
and I'm still wearing an evil eye horn and a scapular and a red
ribbon safety pinned to my bra that I've worn every day
of my life for as long as I can remember? The Italian superstition
of the evil eye horn protects us from people who wish us harm,
and the scapular is from my early days in the Catholic Church,
and my red ribbon that I have been told will protect me
from the malevolent forces in the universe. The officer is moving
her hand over my body. I can't get the words out to explain.
and she says, "Here let me see." She pulls the neck of my shirt
and looks inside my blouse, and I am not ashamed to have her see
my breast, but rather to have her spot the clump of red ribbon,
the old scapular, the gold evil eye horn, and the safety pin
that attaches it to my bra. "Oh," she says, and I know she thinks
I'm wacky for believing these charms can protect me as I believed
in them when I was a little girl and my mother pinned them
to my undershirt, and although I know it's stupid, I wear them
anyway, every day, moving them from a dirty bra to a clean one,
never going out without them. I even have about fourteen red
jackets and scarves and bracelets and necklaces, that color,
some part of me believes, will lead me safely through the perilous
world, and even past the officer who might think I'm crazy,
but waved me through anyway.

TRAVELING LONG DISTANCES

How quickly time travels in a world that once was still
and quiet as a pond in August, days stretching lazily

ahead of me, but now, traveling long distances each week
down highways toward you and away, days,

hours, minutes roll away from me like a ball that increases
its speed, as it rolls downhill, what magician

is this who makes the months vanish, years, birthdays
opening toward me in a crazed circle, and I caught in

the frantic journey from one place to the next and back
again. One day I enter the house and look out

the big window into the side yard that was always
filled with trees and bushes and wildflowers and find

instead that our neighbor has brought in huge cranes
and buzz saws and cut down everything. All that

remains is sawdust, all gone—one-hundred-year-old
oaks, the dogwood tree, the Japanese cherry, lilac

bushes, forsythia—all the vegetation by which
I marked the world's turning and instead I am left

with this moon surface, flattened and ugly, barren
of all that was once alive and growing. Each time

I look out across that emptiness where before so much was,
I think of my own life and how much more

thread is left on the ball of time fate allotted to me,
and the way, no matter what, nothing can slow down

its unwinding.

YOU NEED TO CHANGE

My friend tells me, "You need to change. You're going to kill yourself
with all the running around you do." "I'm not a shrink," she says,
"but you need to see someone." I know she's right. I know I take on
more than I should, know I say yes to too many extra things
as though I have to keep proving something to myself, to the world.
I know but isn't there something in me, some genetic code racing
through my life like road runner, and if I stopped, what
would I give up? Not my students at Binghamton, whom I love,
not the Poetry Center, not the readings and workshops. I think I could
go to a shrink from now until doomsday and my need to excel, to keep
moving no matter how tired I am, is hardwired into my brain, and though
I'd like to please my friend who is a Buddhist and is always going
on two-week retreats where she refuses to answer the phone or have visitors,
there's something electric and exciting I find in all this movement that
I can't give up and don't want to. All those years when you were sick,
all those years when I ran away from everything about your illness I could
not face, driving back and forth between Binghamton and New Jersey
so I could go back to our house crammed with health aides and medicine
and hospital equipment and smile and be kind, each movement away
a respite from being unable to hold you up; in the end, you became
the man I could not look at without wanting to cry, the man whom
I soothed and comforted and only in running away for a few days
to another place could I find the courage to confront all that we lost
and could never hope to find again, except in memory, where you are
still young and healthy, where we can still sit at a campsite on top
of a mountain in New Mexico, your arms around my shoulders,
while the stars in that huge sky glowed for us and for us alone.

The Poet Tells Me

The poet tells me there was a ghost in the cellar
where he slept when he visited another poet.
The ghost wouldn't let him sleep. My ghosts,

my old loves, comfort me. They arrive in 3 a.m. dark
and their hands stroke my hair or touch my cheek.
My mother, though she's been dead nineteen years,
visits more often. She promised she'd come to me
and she has. I imagine I cry in her arms.

Then my father arrives, asks if I've been watching
Murder She Wrote as we did in the evenings
when I visited him in those years after Mom died,

and then my sister sits on the edge of the bed.
She has been gone ten years already,
though she was only sixty-two when she died.

My husband has only been dead six months. He hasn't left
the house yet. I swear he is there with me all the time.
I don't think he's ready to cross over. When he was dying,

he saw all my dead and his own—his mother, father,
grandmothers, even my mother and father.
They came to sit with him. "What did they say," I ask.

"Oh they came to keep me company
so I wouldn't be afraid."

THE STRANGE HOUSE OF THE PAST

Moving through the strange house
    of the past
        the black ink of midnight

what I want is dangerous

    the sound the wind makes,
      a portrait of the world
        in soft orange or blood red.

I dream my cousin teaches me
    how to balance in a kayak
      though I am terrified of water.

In the finished basement where
    I first made love, I learn now to tell
      a rose from a frog, how to break my heart.

Why does the world reek of death and violence?
    In the changing light of the past who
      we were rises up to confront us

We cannot smile or laugh,
    our faces crumple.
      What we want is too dangerous

    to hold or touch.

WATCHING THE SEA

From the hotel balcony in Del Ray Beach, the sea
heaves and whirls, strewing white foam as it crashes
against the shore and the palm fronds bend backwards
in the wind. Later the storm passes and the palms
do their easy slow dance. The water turns a blue so bright
it is like the eyes of black-haired men in Sicily,
their eyes, deep as sapphires, set off by dark skies.
How soothing the calm sea, the sound of it rising
and falling like a whisper or a lullaby. I breathe in
the salt air, soft wind off the water,
the open, endless sky.

I WANT TO NAME THEM ALL

The glaciers are melting in Juneau, Alaska. Even the bees
are vanishing. The hurricane surges ashore and washes
out houses and cars and people for miles along the coast.
Seaside Heights lost its boardwalk and rides; its roller
coaster crouches in the middle of the ocean like a huge, twisted
erector set. The parking lots at the mall are full of cars.
All the toys and clothes and shoes and cars won't soothe us.
What happened to the shimmering quality of light I remember
when I was a child? What happened to the stars
that used to swirl in big chunks through the Paterson sky
like the stars in the van Gogh painting? How could we take
a perfect world and ruin it the way we have with all our wanting
of all the things that make the air unfit to breathe,
the water unfit to drink?

THEY CALL IT FRACKING

They call it fracking, a word that sounds obscene,
to describe fracturing the Marcellus Shale to get
at the natural gas found under the earth's surface.

The people who favor it say it will be done anyway
and the landowners might as well get the money.
The environmentalists say it will pollute the water and air.

In Pennsylvania, the Republican governor says we need
less regulation. The Republican senator says it will bring in
money and jobs. But, if we can't drink the water or breathe
the air, what good will all the money and natural gas and jobs

do us? More fluctuating temperatures and heat waves and violent
rainstorms. I look at the hills and mountains and think
of drilling down to the center of the earth because we are
so besotted with what we must have, what we need, the cash

registers of the world *kachinging, kachinging* and what will we do
with all those shoes and coats and washing machines and cars
when we can no longer breathe?

NEW JERSEY POEM

In New Jersey, with one of the highest cancer
rates in the nation, with its brownfields
and chemical dumps, with its rivers that reek
of death and floating sewage, with its air tainted

by the coal-burning plants in Ohio, with its towns
where all the trees are dying, there are
moments still when I can look beyond
the surface of all the ruin we have brought

to the earth, and see again some of the world
I remember, the daisies and Black-eyed Susans
that seeded the vacant lots of my childhood,
the sky crammed full of stars, the air

so clean I would breathe it in and sigh, the snow
that fell in thick flakes that we ate sprinkled
with sugar and coffee after we scooped it
from the ground into cups. If the air and earth

were already destroyed then we didn't know,
licking this fresh-fallen snow off a spoon,
unaware that the world we were given
was not the one we'd pass on.

LISA MONTGOMERY SPEAKS

"Woman Accused of Stealing Baby Appears in Court"
CNN, 12/21/04

I saw you first at a dog show, the one in Blakely, Missouri.
I made my way toward you, your belly prominent under
your t-shirt. I do not ask you when your baby is due. I do
not tell you of my own three children, stillborn. We exchange
email addresses. I say I am interested in buying one of the Jack
Russell Terriers you breed. I pull you in, make you feel safe.

I make one appointment to pick up a dog from you. I break it.
Finally, the day is set. I will drive from Melvern, Kansas to your
house in Skidmore, Missouri. Your baby will be born in two
weeks. I can barely breathe. "I'm Lisa Montgomery," I say.
You ask me in. When you turn to lead me into your kitchen,
I am ready. I strangle you, stab you five times; you fall
on your tile floor. I turn you over slice

open your belly, lift out what I came for. What am I
without a child? All my children die before they are born,
but not this one, this one I clean off and wrap in the blankets
I brought with me and carry her away. She is mine. What am I
if I do not have a child? When I get back home I tell
my husband that the baby is ours. I tell my neighbors.

I carry the child with me wherever I go. This child is mine.
What am I without her but an empty husk, a barren woman?
I must give my husband this child. I must have her. When they
come to get me, I kick the policeman. I scream and sob. They tear
the child away from me.

I see my husband's shocked face. Even when they have
forced me into the back seat of the police cruiser, even when

71

we pull away, my neighbors, my husband staring, even when
I realize they will never let me have her, and all my planning,
everything I did to get her, is meaningless, even then, I hope
that I can turn back to the time when I held her

and she was mine.

THIS IS THE WAY WE GO TO WAR

This is the way we go to war,
with phrases like Operation
Iraqi freedom designed
to obscure that we are attacking
a country that hasn't attacked us.

This is the way we go to war
with our shock and awe strategy,
repeated ten thousand times a day
on CNN and the image
in the background of the bombs
exploding on Baghdad, "Awesome.
Stupendous," the announcer says.

This is the way we go to war
with the image of Baghdad's
buildings and mosque obscured
by huge flowers of fire,
eerie firecrackers lighting up
the night sky.

This is the way we go to war
with fresh-faced soldiers weighed
down by one-hundred pound packs
and the patriotic words they utter
and with the father of the dead black marine
so angry he is almost crying.
"This war took my son. This war took
my son. It's not right," he says,
his voice shaking, the young soldier's
picture set into a little square
on the TV screen.

This is the way we go to war,
the announcers, like cheerleaders,
watch via video phones,
the columns of fire rising above the city
and they keep on talking about
our awesome power, and I think
of a child playing army and knocking
down bunkers and imitating
the noises guns make.

This is the way we go to war,
"We can't let foreigners do that to us!"
a man on TV says, but in Iraq we are
the foreigners and look what we are
doing, look what we are doing
when we go to war.

Deer Hunt in Princeton, NJ

On TV, I watch deer leap out of the woods.
The hunters in their plaid caps and shotguns
chase them. "The Deer hunt in Princeton
was a success," the newscaster says. Behind him,

the lithe terrified bodies of deer startle
through underbrush, "Four hundred deer were killed
in the last three days," the newscaster shouts
happily into his microphone.

Behind him a deer falls to the ground in slow motion,
an enormous red flower opening in his side,
staining the earth around him. "The deer
had become a nuisance," the announcer says.

I think of driving through New Jersey and seeing
land that used to be forests growing now instead
huge million dollar mansions, monuments to our idea
of success and not a tree in sight, as though

someone came through with a gigantic blade
and sawed through a forest in a day, putting up
manor houses, imitation of course, with twenty rooms
and four car garages and no room at all

for trees or deer. I remember driving home
one night at midnight on a deserted Morris County road
and stopping to let a herd of deer cross.
Delicate and graceful in moonlight,

they moved past me in no hurry at all as though
they were walking across a small dirt path
in the country and not a main road
through the suburbs that spread faster

than kudzu through New Jersey. In Princeton,
the hunters are proud they have killed off
400 deer. Next year, how many will die
to make way for more houses

with seven bathrooms no family
could possibly need?

THE GIANT SINKHOLE

This morning I read in the newspaper about a man from Florida,
Jeff Ross, who went to bed last night about 11 p.m., thinking
of his job, all the things he needed to accomplish the next day,
when he felt the ground tremble and give way. A boom louder
than any bomb sounded, and his body, his bed, his bureau,
his chair, all fell into the giant sinkhole that had opened
under his bedroom. His brother ran into the room and leaped
into the hole, but he could not find his brother, and had
to be pulled out by firemen. The police seal the house off.
No one is allowed inside. "Too unstable," they say. They're sure
Jeff Ross is dead, buried under earth and cement and rubble.
I think for a moment of my neighbor, the one who loves classical
music and concerts, the one who lived in the same house since 1972,
the one who climbed the stairs in his house and got into bed,
the same bed he'd slept in for so long. The storm was violent,
but he wasn't afraid. The big oak in his backyard came crashing
down. It was more than a hundred years old, and it landed right
on top of him. The police say, "He never knew what hit him."

Listening In

In the breakfast room at the Hampton Inn in Vestal, NY,
I overhear a man, ordinary looking, clean blue shirt,
sweater vest, khaki slacks, loafers, this man
his face calm and clean shaven says, "Bob decided
not to shoot Obama." I pretend I don't hear him,
though his words are sharper than the sunlight
pouring through the tall windows and to avoid
the blades of sunlight, I squeeze my eyes shut.
It makes me think of my first day of high school,
freshman year, proud in my red plaid, pleated
wool skirt, my broadcloth shirt, my bobby sox
and saddle shoes, a look I copied from the pages
of *Seventeen* magazine, when the bus driver looked

at me, and said "Oh you little meatball, you juicy
meatball. Oh, oh." His hot eyes burned
my skin, but I kept on walking towards a seat in the back,
my face scorched with shame, my mind scrambling
to figure out why he looked at me
as though I were something he wanted to devour.
I who had so carefully dressed my slender body in clothes
meant to be middle class and safe, what had that bus driver
seen in me that caused that flash of heat. It was my sister,
big-breasted and sexy, who often had men stare at her,
but I at thirteen, was still a little girl trying to be a picture
of what a fifties girl was supposed to be, and even now,
so many years later, I don't know what he meant
or what he wanted. I only know, that sometimes,
like that day and today in the Hampton Inn, the only thing
to do is to pretend you haven't heard a truth so terrifying
you don't want to know or understand.

AFTER MY READING IN NEW YORK CITY

After my reading a young woman in jeans
and a lavender tee shirt approaches me.
"You insulted my profession," she says.
"What profession?" I ask. "I'm a prostitute."
I apologize to her, and do a lot of backpedalling.
"You know people think we're prostitutes because
we like sex. We do it for the money," she says.
I apologize again, and then make it worse by saying,
"I think your profession might be dangerous. You are
taking care of yourself, aren't you?" and I pat her
on the arm, turn myself into her grandmother.
"Oh yes," she says, "the older women tell us what to do."
It isn't often that I can't think of anything to say,
but at the moment, no more words come, not of apology
or excuse or explanation. Like a car that has stalled,
I sputter out another apology. When I am leaving, I wave at her,
though she is looking at me as though she'd like to run me over,
and I wonder what planet I come from that I think waving at her
would be appropriate, just like I blow a kiss to my Hasidic student
even after he jumped away from me earlier in the day when
I tried to hug him and he shouted, "No, only my wife is allowed
to touch me." My friend says, "Why is it whenever you get near
him, you touch him, you touch his arm, reach out toward him?
He may have to go upstairs and take a shower when you do that."
What little devil inside me, made me blow him a kiss when he
is presenting at an academic conference, and I can only hope
he doesn't have to take a bath again. He'll end up being
the cleanest man at the conference, thanks to me.

Manhattan Cab Story

The other night in New York City I tried to climb into
one of those cabs that is a like a van and I grabbed
onto the handle, lifted one leg up into the cab. I started
to lift the other but couldn't make it and I began to fall
backward, the blacktop gleaming and icy beneath me,
my ass moving inexorably toward it, me calling, "Help, help,"
and the doorman running toward me and cradling
my wide behind in his two hands. He lifted me into the seat.

The cab driver got out of the cab and began to scream at me
in heavily accented English, "Get out, get out! I won't take you.
It's not safe." I try to argue but realize it is as futile as arguing
with the cab driver in St. Petersburg, Russia, who insisted
we owed him $100 for a five minute ride. I slide myself
out of the cab, carefully, as a carton of eggs, extra large,

and the doorman screams at me, "Why did you get out
of the cab?" "He wouldn't let me stay in his cab," I say,
and now everyone in front of the hotel and on the street
has stopped to stare at the scene unfolding before them.
"I won't get you another cab," the doorman shouts.

A young couple out on a Valentine's date stare at us.
The girl says, "Can't we take her in our cab?" Her eyes
are large and kind. Her boyfriend looks annoyed.
I say, "No, no you go on your date. Happy Valentine's Day.
I'll get a cab at the corner. I'm okay," and as I walk
toward 8th Avenue I feel eyes watching me, an unwilling
contestant on a really mean reality show, and although
I get a cab that I can easily climb into, I am wearing
a cloak of humiliation and worry.

Ten Years Ago

Ten years ago what I didn't know was how much it is possible
to lose in ten years—my father, sister, husband all passed
over the bridge to heaven and I on this side calling their names.
My own body growing weaker, my sense of time fleeting
and of me losing a bit more each day. Ten years ago I could walk
for blocks without getting tired or dizzy or out of breath, and ten years
from now, what can I expect, what can I hope to have kept? I try not
to think of what else it would be possible to lose, especially today
when I'm feeling so discouraged and tired, the hours of this day
as much as I can carry without dropping. My mother appears
to me scolding, "Oh, stop complaining." I imagine her saying,
"Look how lucky you've been," and I feel the blessings
I have been granted cover me with their exquisite light,
grateful for this glorious sunny day, grateful for the tulips' yellow
mouths, grateful for the softening of the world into spring, grateful
for the poems that spill out of me onto paper, grateful for the art I create,
grateful for my daughter's voice, grateful for my son's solid presence,
grateful for the students who surround me on this April day, even after
the sun retreats behind clouds and the room grows darker, the students'
poems provide the light in this room, the fire.

RAPUNZEL

Think what it must have been like for her, caged
in her tower, the small window cut into dark
stone, the hours it took to brush

and untangle her hair, waiting for the prince
to come so she could let down her hair
and he could climb up to her room.

Think what it must have been like for her, lonely
and starved for attention like the girls now
who stare into their bathroom mirrors, brushing

and combing their hair, applying perfume, mascara, skin
softener, make-up, all in honor of the man who will stand
outside their window, their beauty a braid lowered

to the outside world, their lives spent, breathless
and silent, waiting for a man to rescue them,
as though their own hands were not strong enough,

their own hearts not brave enough, their own minds
not quick enough for them to save themselves.

My Granddaughter Loves Old Movies

My granddaughter loves 30s and 40s movies, loves watching
"Singing in the Rain" over and over again.

My granddaughter loves vintage clothes and clothes
in general. She takes photographs of herself in the clothes
and writes a blog about it.

My granddaughter loves books, music and spends way too
much time alone.

My granddaughter is striking—tall, slender, graceful.
In photographs she looks like a model.

My granddaughter copies hair styles from 30s movies
and takes photographs of herself by setting up her camera
and running to a spot to pose. The photographs are art; they're
compositions of light and shadow, perfectly balanced.

My granddaughter loves me and I love her. "You're so brave,
Grandma," she says. "You don't care what anyone thinks
about you." I say, "When I was your age, I was
a coward. I was always skulking into corners to hide. I think
you're brave," I tell her. "You get dressed in vintage clothes
when everyone else is wearing jeans and t-shirts."

My granddaughter is as naïve as I was in the 1950s. Maybe
it was safer to be naïve back then. Now, I am afraid for her.
I want to ask her if she knows about birth control and STD's.
I ask if her mother's talked to her about sex. She says no.
I am horrified because my granddaughter has dates with her
first boyfriend. When she breaks up with him, I am relieved.

My friend tells me, "Oh, she can get all the information
she needs on the web." I think of myself at her age,
a freshman in college, my first real boyfriend, and the things
he talked me into doing that were neither safe nor prudent.
We made love for the first time in a construction shack
on a site where his uncle worked. He pushed aside
the office supplies on a table, and I let him. The table
was hard against my bony back. It was snowing
outside. I was terrified we'd be caught, but I didn't say no.
I am afraid for my granddaughter, so far away from me,
how can I protect her when in my own past I made love
on a splintery table and after that anywhere
he wanted—in the parking lot of All Pro Bowling Lanes
and parked in the street, three streets down from my house,
and in the park and in the back seat of his Plymouth
in Lover's Lane in Englewood Cliffs, with the lights
of New York across the river which were beautiful
but didn't make me feel any safer from the police
who patrolled the lane, afraid they'd shine their light
on us and I'd be caught half naked.

My granddaughter, I know she has to learn for herself,
about loss, love, betrayal, I know I can't protect her.
No one can. I worry from a distance and imagine her living
in her fantasy world, watching "Singing in the Rain,"
where sex is never mentioned and everything is light
and airy and unreal.

ON MODIGLIANI'S WOMEN

I think of Modigliani's women, how tall and slender
they are, their heads, with their short hair and slightly
startled eyes, their long necks. I always loved them,
though I never looked like that myself, even when
I was still young and slim.

My granddaughter looks like them, she is five-foot-eight,
weighs 104 pounds, max. Earlier this year, she had her hair cut
into a pixie cut, or that's what we called it when I was a girl.
I opened her Facebook page and there she was with this very
short hair cut and long dangly earrings shaped like feathers
that emphasize her long neck. She could have stepped out
of a Modigliani painting.

I'm worried about her, worried that she places food on her plate
but only moves it around. When she gets up she says she has
to exercise for two or three hours. The other day I see on her
Facebook page that she's posted a new picture. She's even thinner
than she was before. I always loved Modigliani's paintings, wanting
to step inside the long narrow bodies, but of course,

we can't change what we are, can't become the body we wish
we had. What does my granddaughter see when she looks
in the mirror? It took me so long to stop wanting to step
inside someone else's skin, so long to be grateful to walk flat
footed, confident into my life, this woman I've become,
this woman, brave, certain, who moves forward,
never stops, never allows anything to get in her way.
See how she leaves behind that image of the girl
in the Modigliani painting, glad to be what
she has become: that laugh, that chunky body,
those pounding feet.

NAMES

My mother's name was Angelina Schiavo, my father's Arturo
Mazziotti. His father was Alessandro; his mother Laura Cortiglia.
I do not know my mother's parents' names. This is an immigrant's
story, so much of the past lost and never to be regained.
My children remember their grandmothers and grandfathers
and that is as far back as they go. My grandchildren know me
and their grandfather, but not very well. My mother came
to America in 1936 when she was twenty-three. She left her mother
behind in San Mauro, and never saw her again. My son and his wife,
my grandchildren, live in Dallas now. I try to be a presence in their lives,
try to make them remember me, exchanging emails and favorite poems
with my granddaughter. I wish they lived near me. My parents
had to leave their parents behind so I never had grandparents, knew them
only as blue airmail letters. We need to know our ancestors, that line
of traits and blood that makes us the people we are. The last time I visited
my grandchildren, I started to sing—off-key of course—and grabbed
my sixteen-year-old grandson and said, "Let's dance." At first, he looked
at me as though I had lost my mind and then he let me twirl him around
the room. This grandson whose broad shoulders and solid body are
as steadfast and loyal as he is, and my granddaughter, tall, slender, graceful,
who looks nothing like me but who carries a book with her wherever she goes,
who also loves to write, who knows what other parts of her come from
those people who came before us, even the ones
whose names I never knew.

BIANCHERIA AND MY MOTHER

As a girl, my mother embroidered linen towels
with her initials, tablecloths and linen slips
and nightgowns, placed them neatly in a trunk.
When she married my father, she brought the trunk

to America in the hold of the ship where she traveled
in steerage. She was six-months pregnant and sick
most of the way over, but on the day the ship arrived
in New York, she tells me she was so excited she got

dressed in her best dress, blue with a white collar,
and a blue hat and waved and waved to my father
who waited on the dock for her. Before she left Italy,
my father's mother gave her appliquéd tablecloths

she'd made of fine linen, the stitches so delicate
and perfect they were a work of art. My mother, like
the other Italian immigrant women, knew how to sew
so she got a job sewing the sleeves in coats by hand.

The factory would drop the coats off first thing
in the morning and pick up the ones she had sewn
the day before. It was called piecework. Later, when we,
her children, were old enough to be in school, she worked

at Ferraro's Coat Factory, doing the same work, but paid
a penny more for each piece that she sewed. The whole time
we were growing up, my mother bought sheets
and towels for my sister and myself, bought a metal trunk

for each of us, and began to save the *biancheria*.
She taught us how to embroider so that we would

have dresser scarves and towels that we had embroidered
with our initials or with pre-printed flowers. For my mother

that *biancheria* was our dowry, something she felt she had
to give us. When I married I had this huge trunk that I carted
wherever I went, the sheets my mother bought for me
with the pennies she earned sewing in that factory were 100%

cotton and needed to be ironed. I was 100% lazy
and not domestic and bought permanent press sheets
for myself, her sheets packed in the trunk like an accusation.
I still have the embroidered towels and dresser scarves
and tablecloths, but a few years ago, I emptied the trunk
of all those sheets I knew I'd never use and let my daughter
sell them at a garage sale, and as I lifted them out, I thought
of my mother, sewing those coats for years, piles of basting

thread covering her feet, and of what we can pass on,
and what we can't, and the *biancheria* I have saved
for my daughter and how much else we give
when we try to pass it on.

MY MOTHER TELLS US STORIES OF SAN MAURO

Inside me, I hear the voices of the women who came before
me, my mother and grandmother, my aunts, my sister,
all of them speaking that Cilentano dialect until their words
blend together and form the beat I move to, the lessons

we learned through the way they worked, the things
and people they loved, the work they did to earn money,
the houses they cleaned and polished, the meals
they cooked, heavy with garlic and basil and oregano,

picked fresh from their gardens, their whispers become
a thread of sound inside me, firm and strong
as the wax-coated thread my mother used to sew
the lining in coats at Ferraro Coat factory. These were not

fancy women, not delicate like silk thread, but tough
and utilitarian and used to hard work and doing
without, my mother carrying San Mauro in her blood and in
her heart so that she could teach us that place we had never

seen, teach us how to weave that same thread, the one that
I use to pleat together my past and that I twist into a rope,
strong as a suspension bridge that leads my daughter home.
Women have done this forever stitching this strong thread

from one generation to the next, teaching their daughters
to be women, not by what they say,
but what they do.

This Is a Love Song, a Work Song, a Song of Grief

I imagine the long line of my ancestors working the fields
in those ancient stone villages on the top of the mountain
in San Mauro, Italy, the houses huddled together and strung
down the hillside, and the fields built into plots like steps up
the sides of steep mountains. I think of them making their way
in early morning to their farms, working all day, singing
to keep themselves from thinking about the ache
in their stooped shoulders, their tired muscles, the sweat
that trickled inside the bandanas they tied around their heads.

This is a love song, a work song, a song of grief,
for all the years of hard labor in that blazing Mediterranean sun,
a song for the work that never ended, a song for the crops
that blossomed and bore fruit, the harvest that kept their families
alive all winter. When the wind chilled their bones, they moved
their animals into the barns attached to their houses, the children
sleeping six to a bed, the pigs snorting, the goats' hoarse cries.

This is a love song, a work song, a song of grief for the fireplace
in the kitchen in which they cooked their food, the outhouse,
the tin washboard, the hard life they led and did not complain,
a song for the women who bore children in the fields,
who worked until the child was born, and then rose again
to work, the crops needing to be harvested and preserved before
winter and the lean times and the family working together
in those fields and kitchens, the parents, grandparents
and the children, all learning this song of love,
this song of work, this song of grief.

ANCESTORS' SONG

I come from a long line of women, who never gave up,
who knew how to work hard, not stop. I imagine them
working in the fields built into the mountainside
in San Mauro, the fields which they walked to each morning,
and returned each night to their stone houses to cook
and wash and clean. For me they will always wear black
dresses like the mourning dresses my mother wore for years.
Each time a relative died in Italy, my mother would wear
the black mourning dress for at least a year. That was what
she was taught to do as a girl in San Mauro and that's what
she did long after she left San Mauro behind.

When I visit San Mauro, I see my first cousins look just like
me, though I never met them before. We are short, squat,
sturdy. They are physically stronger than I am, still work in
their gardens and kitchens for hours each day, but in so many
ways, we are alike. My cousin Lillina's sardonic humor so like
my mother's, my other cousin Anna's exquisite handiwork
and the neat precision with which she folds the delicate
napkin and serves her homemade cake. It's as though I've
met them all before. My mother's stories kept them alive
as I try to keep my parents alive for my children
and grandchildren.

In my daughter I see my mother—my daughter who works
for twenty-four hours straight on a paper or a book,
my daughter who demands perfection from herself,
my daughter who does not know how to sit still
or to pamper herself.

And I know that the one thing I wish I had not given her
is this drive to succeed, to be better than she was the day
before, no time for long days on a beach, no time for

vacation, no time for dreaming, only this, this need to keep
on going even when she's so tired her eyes look dazed, to
keep on going the way my mother did, the way I always do,
and I want to erase that part of our ancestors I passed to her,
though I tell her to take a vacation, to rest, she only
has to look at the way I live to know that I have not
been able to take my own advice, all those women
that came before us beating in my blood, that song I know
without ever having heard the words, just as my daughter knows,
and nothing I can do or say to save her.

THINKING BACK, I REMEMBER MY MOTHER
San Mauro, Cilento, August, 2006

Thinking back, I remember my mother, how energy crackled
off her like a brush fire, remember her laugh, head thrown back,
remember the way she was always working,

the way she couldn't even watch TV without crocheting so many
blankets that all the children and grandchildren had two or three
apiece. And I think of this summer in San Mauro,

the small mountain village in southern Italy where she grew up,
think of sitting with her sister's children who are close to my age
now, my first cousins, the ones I had never met

before this summer, see us sitting on Anna's terrace with its view
of the mountains and the sea, see us having our photographs
taken, our arms around each other, our genes

evident in how similar we are, the sound of their voices and their
accents and their faces bring my mother back to me as though she
were there with us though she is dead fifteen

years now. Anna takes me into her house to show me its rooms
and to give me a delicate hand-made linen scarf that is so
beautifully ironed and folded that again my mother is with us,
my mother who despaired of my domestic abilities, who took my
clothes to her house to wash for me, and told me they were so
dirty she had to wash them three times to get them clean,

my mother who, like these San Mauro women, was a brilliant cook,
how artistic she was with food, serving it so carefully, once she told
me you had to serve lots of different foods at once so you'd

please the eye, just like my cousin Anna serves me her special
chocolate dessert, chocolate with almonds on a thin china dish
with a handmade linen napkin,

and how happy I am at this moment to be here with my cousins
and my daughter and Anna's daughter, sure that
my mother is with us.

IN THESE SOUTHERN ITALIAN MOUNTAINS

To Maria and Mario Volpe,
San Mauro, Cilento, Campagnia

On this clear July morning, the skin of the world
is scrubbed and shining. The lemons are big yellow
jewels in the trees; the grapes on the grape arbor
hang in clusters so perfectly formed they could be
a work of art, and I am sitting on my cousin Maria's
terrace. Flowers grow all around us in plaster pots
that line the walls. I feel all the taut strings of my life
loosen, the air smooth as scented cream on my face,

and for one moment in these southern Italian mountains,
I could almost be one of the enormous butterflies
that light on the flowers and fly off, so weightless am I
and happy, staring off at the mountains opposite
where San Mauro, my mother's home town, is strung
like a necklace across the mountain tops. Maria brings
me an espresso and pastry she made just for me,

because I mentioned my mother used to make it
and so she got up at 5 a.m. to start the elaborate
process and finished at 12:30, presenting me with a huge
tray of *pastechelle* drizzled with honey and sprinkles
and I feel welcomed in the place, as though my mother
and father were here with me, leading me home.

ABOUT THE AUTHOR

MARIA MAZZIOTTI GILLAN is a recipient of the 2011 Barnes & Noble Writers for Writers Award from *Poets & Writers*, and the 2008 American Book Award for her book, *All That Lies Between Us* (Guernica Editions). She is the Founder/Executive Director of the Poetry Center at Passaic County Community College in Paterson, NJ, and editor of the *Paterson Literary Review*. She is also Director of the Creative Writing Program and Professor of Poetry at Binghamton University-SUNY.

Mazziotti Gillan has published seventeen books, including: *What We Pass On: Collected Poems 1980-2009* (Guernica Editions), *The Place I Call Home* and *The Silence in an Empty House* (NYQ Books), and *Writing Poetry to Save Your Life: How to Find the Courage to Tell Your Stories* (MiroLand, Guernica). With her daughter Jennifer, she is co-editor of four anthologies.

Visit her website at *www.mariagillan.com*.

Bordighera Press is an imprint of Bordighera, Incorporated, an independently owned not-for-profit
scholarly organization that has no legal affiliation with the University of Central Florida or with
The John D. Calandra Italian American Institute, Queens College/CUNY.

MARIA FAMÀ, *Looking For Cover*, Vol. 45, Poetry, $12

ANTHONY VALERIO, *Toni Cade Bambara's One Sicilian Night*, Vol. 44, Poetry, $10

EMANUEL CARNEVALI, Dennis Barone, Ed., *Furnished Rooms*, Vol. 43, Poetry, $14

BRENT ADKINS, et al., Ed., *Shifting Borders, Negotiating Places*, Vol. 42, Proceedings, $18

GEORGE GUIDA, *Low Italian*, Vol. 41, Poetry, $11

GARDAPHÈ, GIORDANO, TAMBURRI, *Introducing Italian Americana*, Vol. 40, Italian/American Studies, $10

DANIELA GIOSEFFI, *Blood Autumn/Autunno di sangue*, Vol. 39, Poetry, $15/$25

FRED MISURELLA, *Lies to Live by*, Vol. 38, Stories, $15

STEVEN BELLUSCIO, *Constructing a Bibliography*, Vol. 37, Italian Americana, $15

ANTHONY JULIAN TAMBURRI, Ed., *Italian Cultural Studies 2002*, Vol. 36, Essays, $18

BEA TUSIANI, *con amore*, Vol. 35, Memoir, $19

FLAVIA BRIZIO-SKOV, Ed., *Reconstructing Societies in the Aftermath of War*, Vol. 34, History, $30

TAMBURRI, et al., Eds., *Italian Cultural Studies 2001*, Vol. 33, Essays, $18

ELIZABETH G. MESSINA, Ed., *In Our Own Voices*, Vol. 32, Italian/American Studies, $25

STANISLAO G. PUGLIESE, *Desperate Inscriptions*, Vol. 31, History, $12

HOSTERT & TAMBURRI, Eds., *Screening Ethnicity*, Vol. 30, Italian/American Culture, $25

G. PARATI & B. LAWTON, Eds., *Italian Cultural Studies*, Vol. 29, Essays, $18

HELEN BAROLINI, *More Italian Hours*, Vol. 28, Fiction, $16

FRANCO NASI, Ed., *Intorno alla Via Emilia*, Vol. 27, Culture, $16

ARTHUR L. CLEMENTS, *The Book of Madness & Love*, Vol. 26, Poetry, $10

JOHN CASEY, et al., *Imagining Humanity*, Vol. 25, Interdisciplinary Studies, $18

ROBERT LIMA, *Sardinia/Sardegna*, Vol. 24, Poetry, $10

DANIELA GIOSEFFI, *Going On*, Vol. 23, Poetry, $10

ROSS TALARICO, *The Journey Home*, Vol. 22, Poetry, $12

EMANUEL DI PASQUALE, *The Silver Lake Love Poems*, Vol. 21, Poetry, $7

JOSEPH TUSIANI, *Ethnicity*, Vol. 20, Poetry, $12

JENNIFER LAGIER, *Second Class Citizen*, Vol. 19, Poetry, $8

FELIX STEFANILE, *The Country of Absence*, Vol. 18, Poetry, $9

PHILIP CANNISTRARO, *Blackshirts*, Vol. 17, History, $12

LUIGI RUSTICHELLI, Ed., *Seminario sul racconto*, Vol. 16, Narrative, $10

LEWIS TURCO, *Shaking the Family Tree*, Vol. 15, Memoirs, $9

LUIGI RUSTICHELLI, Ed., *Seminario sulla drammaturgia*, Vol. 14, Theater/Essays, $10

FRED GARDAPHÈ, *Moustache Pete is Dead! Long Live Moustache Pete!*, Vol. 13, Oral Literature, $10

JONE GAILLARD CORSI, *Il libretto d'autore, 1860–1930*, Vol. 12, Criticism, $17

HELEN BAROLINI, *Chiaroscuro: Essays of Identity*, Vol. 11, Essays, $15

PICARAZZI & FEINSTEIN, Eds., *An African Harlequin in Milan*, Vol. 10, Theater/Essays, $15

JOSEPH RICAPITO, *Florentine Streets & Other Poems*, Vol. 9, Poetry, $9

FRED MISURELLA, *Short Time*, Vol. 8, Novella, $7

NED CONDINI, *Quartettsatz*, Vol. 7, Poetry, $7

ANTHONY JULIAN TAMBURRI, Ed., *Fuori: Essays by Italian/American Lesbians and Gays*, Vol. 6, Essays, $10

ANTONIO GRAMSCI, P. Verdicchio, Trans. & Intro. , *The Southern Question*, Vol. 5, Social Criticism, $5

DANIELA GIOSEFFI, *Word Wounds & Water Flowers*, Vol. 4, Poetry, $8

WILEY FEINSTEIN, *Humility's Deceit: Calvino Reading Ariosto Reading Calvino*, Vol. 3, Criticism, $10

PAOLO A. GIORDANO, Ed., *Joseph Tusiani: Poet, Translator, Humanist*, Vol. 2, Criticism, $25

ROBERT VISCUSI, *Oration Upon the Most Recent Death of Christopher Columbus*, Vol. 1, Poetry, $3

www.ingramcontent.com/pod-product-compliance
Lightning Source LLC
LaVergne TN
LVHW041301080426
835510LV00009B/828